PRAYERS AND PROMISES OF JESUS

Copyright © 1980 Lion Publishing
This combined edition © 1990 Lion Publishing

Published by
Lion Publishing plc
Sandy Lane West, Oxford, England
ISBN 0 7459 2602 9
Lion Publishing
1705 Hubbard Avenue, Batavia, Illinois 60510, USA
ISBN 0 7459 2602 9
Albatross Books Pty Ltd
PO Box 320, Sutherland, NSW 2232, Australia
ISBN 0 7324 0624 2

First edition in this format 1990
Paperback edition 1992

A catalogue record for this book is available
from the British Library

Printed and bound in Hong Kong

PRAYERS
AND
PROMISES
OF
JESUS

A LION BOOK

Oxford · Batavia · Sydney

CONTENTS

Prayers of Jesus

Promises of Jesus

PART ONE

PRAYERS
OF
JESUS

Man of prayer

Crowds of people came to hear him
and to be healed of their sicknesses.
But Jesus often withdrew to lonely
places and prayed.

Luke 5:15–16

The hills of Galilee, where Jesus often prayed.

Our Father

Seeing Jesus pray, his disciples asked him to teach
them how to pray. He gave them the pattern prayer
which Christians have used down the centuries.

Our Father in heaven,
hallowed be your name.

God's will, on earth

Your kingdom come,
your will be done

on earth as it is in heaven.

The village of Maloula in Syria.

All we need

Give us today our daily bread.

Forgiveness

Forgive us our debts,
as we also have forgiven our debtors.
And lead us not into temptation,
but deliver us from the evil one.

Matthew 6:9–13

Jesus
gives thanks

When he was faced with five thousand hungry
people, and only five loaves and two fish to feed
them with, Jesus remained unperturbed. Calmly, as
his custom was, he gave God thanks for the food
provided.

Taking the five loaves and the two
fish and looking up to heaven, he
gave thanks and broke the loaves.
Then he gave them to his disciples to
set before the people. He also divided
the two fish among them all. They all
ate and were satisfied.

Mark 6:41–42

Jesus fed the crowds on a hillside in Galilee.

Jesus rejoices

Jesus sent out seventy-two of his followers. They were to go ahead of him, two by two, to every town and place where he was about to go. They were to heal the sick and tell people of God's kingdom: that Jesus had come to begin a new age.
The seventy-two returned with joy, telling how even the demons submitted to them in Christ's name. Jesus shared their joy, praising God:

I praise you, Father, Lord of heaven and earth, because you have hidden these things from the wise and learned, and revealed them to little children. Yes, Father, for this was your good pleasure.

Luke 10:21

Jesus blesses the children

People brought their children to Jesus, wanting him to ask God's blessing on them. When the disciples tried to protect him from their demands, turning people away, Jesus was angry.

'Let the little children come to me, and do not hinder them, for the kingdom of God belongs to such as these. I tell you the truth, anyone who will not receive the kingdom of God like a little child will never enter it.' And he took the children in his arms, put his hands on them and blessed them.

Mark 10:14–16

Lazarus lives

Jesus' friend Lazarus had died. His sisters could not understand why Jesus had not arrived in time to heal him. They had not yet learned that his power extends beyond the grave. Jesus ordered the people to take away the stone that sealed the entrance to the tomb. Then he prayed to God.

'Father, I thank you that you have heard me. I knew that you always hear me, but I said this for the benefit of the people standing here, that they may believe that you sent me.'
When he had said this, Jesus called in a loud voice, 'Lazarus, come out!' The dead man came out, his hands and feet wrapped with strips of linen, and a cloth around his face.
Jesus said to them, 'Take off the grave clothes and let him go.'

John 11:41–44

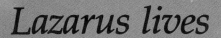

Facing death

Jesus had been speaking to his followers about his coming death. It was necessary for him to die – just as corn must fall to the ground and die to produce new grain. Yet it was hard to face suffering.

Now my heart is troubled, and what shall I say? 'Father, save me from this hour'? No, it was for this very reason I came to this hour. Father, glorify your name!

John 12:27–28

Eternal life

On the eve of his death, in the upper room with the little group of his close friends, Jesus prayed – for himself, for his friends and for all who would believe in him.

Father, the time has come. Glorify your Son, that your Son may glorify you. For you granted him authority over all people that he might give eternal life to all those you have given him. Now this is eternal life: that they may know you, the only true God, and Jesus Christ, whom you have sent.

John 17:1–3

Houses built in traditional style, in a village in Israel.

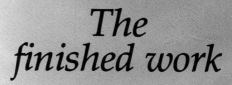

The
finished work

I have brought you glory on earth by completing the work you gave me to do. And now, Father, glorify me in your presence with the glory I had with you before the world began.

John 17:4–5

All one

I am not praying for the world, but for those you have given me, for they are yours. All I have is yours, and all you have is mine. And glory has come to me through them. I will remain in the world no longer, but they are still in

the world, and I am coming to you.
Holy Father, protect them by the
power of your name – the name you
gave me – so that they may be one as
we are one.

John 17:9–11

Women gathering olives in Tunisia.

Kept safe

My prayer is not that you take them
out of the world but that you protect
them from the evil one. They are not
of the world, even as I am not of it.
Sanctify them by the truth; your word
is truth. As you sent me into the
world, I have sent them into the
world.

John 17:15–18

A crowded street in the old city of Jerusalem.

Gethsemane

On the night of his betrayal, Jesus took his friends to a quiet orchard of olive-trees. In great agony of mind, he prayed – about the cup of suffering he was about to drink, the death he was about to die. For he was to take onto his own shoulders the burden of the world's sin.

My Father, if it is possible, may this cup be taken from me. Yet not as I will, but as you will.

Matthew 26:39

An ancient olive-tree in the Garden of Gethsemane.

Forgive them

Outside the city of Jerusalem, at the place called The Skull, Jesus was crucified, between two criminals. At the point of death he prayed for his enemies.

Father, forgive them, for they do not know what they are doing.

Luke 23:34

The Golden Gate and city walls, Jerusalem.

Alone

On the cross, Jesus took on himself the weight of human sin, the horror of separation from God the Father. He cried out in an agony of pain and loneliness.

My God, my God, why have you forsaken me?

Matthew 27:46

Last words

Jesus' dying breath, as he hung on the cross, was a
prayer to God.

Father, into your hands I commit my
spirit.

Luke 23:46

The risen Christ

Two days later, on the first Easter Sunday, two of
Jesus' disciples were walking along a road talking of
Jesus' death and the rumour that he was alive again.
A stranger joined them, and as they reached the
village was invited to stay. It was as he thanked God
for the evening meal that they realized he was Jesus.

When he was at the table with them,
he took bread, gave thanks, broke it
and began to give it to them. Then
their eyes were opened and they
recognized him.

Luke 24:30–31

The ascension

Jesus appeared to his disciples over a period of forty days after his resurrection. When the time came for him to return to his Father, his last action was to pray God's blessing on them all.

When he had led them out to the
vicinity of Bethany, he lifted up his
hands and blessed them. While he
was blessing them, he left them and
was taken up into heaven.

Luke 24:50–51

The village of Bethany, close
to Jerusalem.

PART TWO

PROMISES
OF
JESUS

Kept by God

All that the Father gives me will come to me, and whoever comes to me I will never drive away. For I have come down from heaven not to do my will but to do the will of him who sent me. And this is the will of him who

sent me, that I shall lose none of all that he has given me, but raise them up at the last day. For my Father's will is that everyone who looks to the Son and believes in him shall have eternal life, and I will raise him up at the last day.

John 6:37–40

A child, held safe in a pannier, returns from the fields with her father.

Real happiness

Looking at his disciples, Jesus said:

'Blessed are you who are poor,
for yours is the kingdom of God.
Blessed are you who hunger now,
for you will be satisfied.

Blessed are you who weep now,
for you will laugh.
Blessed are you when men hate you,
when they exclude you and insult you
and reject your name as evil,
because of the Son of Man.
Rejoice in that day and leap for joy,
because great is your reward in heaven.'

Luke 6:20–23

A group of happy children in Jerusalem.

God
will provide

Do not set your heart on what you
will eat or drink; do not worry about
it. For the pagan world runs after all
such things, and your Father knows
that you need them. But seek his
kingdom, and these things will be
given to you as well.

Luke 12:29–31

Food on display in a market at Bergama (ancient
Pergamum) in Turkey.

Living bread

I tell you the truth, he who believes
has everlasting life. I am the bread of
life. Your forefathers ate the manna in
the desert, yet they died. But there is
the bread that comes down from

heaven, which a man may eat and not
die. I am the living bread that came
down from heaven. If a man eats of
this bread, he will live for ever. This
bread is my flesh, which I will give for
the life of the world.

John 6:47–51

A Bedouin woman in Jordan bakes unleavened
bread.

God's infinite care

Are not two sparrows sold for a penny? Yet not one of them will fall to the ground apart from the will of your Father. And even the very hairs of your head are all numbered.

Matthew 10:29–30

A place prepared

Do not let your hearts be troubled. Trust in God; trust also in me. In my Father's house are many rooms; if it were not so, I would have told you. I am going there to prepare a place for you. And if I go and prepare a place for you, I will come back and take you to be with me that you also may be where I am.

John 14:1–3

A scene of tropical beauty, beside Lake Galilee.

Rest

Come to me, all you who are weary
and burdened, and I will give you
rest. Take my yoke upon you and
learn from me, for I am gentle and
humble in heart, and you will find
rest for your souls. For my yoke is
easy and my burden is light.

Matthew 11:28–30

A Turkish farmer rests from his work.

'A hundred times as much'

I tell you the truth . . . no-one who
has left home or brothers or sisters or
mother or father or children or fields
for me and the gospel will fail to
receive a hundred times as much in
this present age (homes, brothers,
sisters, mothers, children and fields –
and with them, persecutions) and in
the age to come, eternal life.

Mark 10:29–30

Gathering in a rich harvest.

Faith

When they came to the crowd, a man approached Jesus and knelt before him. 'Lord, have mercy on my son,' he said. 'He is an epileptic and is suffering greatly. He often falls into the fire or into the water. I brought him to your disciples, but they could not heal him.'

'O unbelieving and perverse generation,' Jesus replied, 'how long shall I stay with you? How long shall I put up with you? Bring the boy here to me.' Jesus rebuked the demon, and

it came out of the boy, and he was
healed from that moment.

Then the disciples came to Jesus in
private and asked, 'Why couldn't we
drive it out?'

He replied, 'Because you have so little
faith. I tell you the truth, if you have
faith as small as a mustard seed, you
can say to this mountain, "Move from
here to there" and it will move.
Nothing will be impossible for you.'

Matthew 17:14–20

The distant mountains are Mt Gerizim and Mt Ebal
in 'Samaria'.

Whatever you ask for

Whatever you ask for in prayer,
believe that you have received it, and
it will be yours.

Mark 11:24

Safe in God's care

My sheep listen to my voice; I know them, and they follow me. I give them eternal life, and they shall never perish; no-one can snatch them out of my hand. My Father, who has given them to me, is greater than all; no-one can snatch them out of my Father's hand. I and the Father are one.

John 10:27–30

A shepherd watches over his flock of sheep.

God's measure

Do not judge, and you will not be judged. Do not condemn, and you will not be condemned. Forgive, and you will be forgiven. Give, and it will be given to you. A good measure, pressed down, shaken together and running over, will be poured into your lap. For with the measure you use, it will be measured to you.

Luke 6:37–38

Beans and nuts sold by measure in the market at Nazareth.

Life-giving water

Everyone who drinks this water will
be thirsty again, but whoever drinks
the water I give him will never thirst.
Indeed, the water I give him will
become in him a spring of water
welling up to eternal life.

John 4:13–14

A pool of water from the spring at Engedi, Israel.

The food that lasts

Do not work for food that spoils, but for food that endures to eternal life, which the Son of Man will give you. On him God the Father has placed his seal of approval.

John 6:27

A Jewish meal being enjoyed out of doors.

'My servant'

I tell you the truth, unless an ear of
wheat falls to the ground and dies, it
remains only a single seed. But if it
dies, it produces many seeds. The
man who loves his life will lose it,
while the man who hates his life in
this world will keep it for eternal life.
Whoever serves me must follow me;
and where I am, my servant also will
be. My Father will honour the one
who serves me.

John 12:24–26

God's
promised power

This is what is written: The Christ will
suffer and rise from the dead on the
third day, and repentance and
forgiveness of sins will be preached in
his name to all nations, beginning at
Jerusalem. You are witnesses of these
things. I am going to send you what
my Father has promised; but stay in
the city until you have been clothed
with power from on high.

Luke 24:46–49

Looking towards the city of Jerusalem.

All truth

When he, the Spirit of truth, comes,
he will guide you into all truth. He
will not speak on his own; he will
speak only what he hears, and he will
tell you what is yet to come.

John 16:13

A candle illuminates the Scriptures.

'I will come to you'

I will not leave you as orphans; I will come to you. Before long, the world will not see me any more, but you will see me. Because I live, you also will live. On that day you will realise that I am in my Father, and you are in me, and I am in you.

John 14:18–20

Sunrise on Lake Galilee.

Jesus' promise from the cross

One of the criminals who hung there hurled insults at him: 'Aren't you the Christ? Save yourself and us!'

But the other criminal rebuked him. 'Don't you fear God,' he said, 'since you are under the same sentence? We are punished justly, for we are getting what our deeds deserve. But this man has done nothing wrong.' Then he said, 'Jesus, remember me when you come into your kingdom.'

Jesus answered him, 'I tell you the truth, today you will be with me in paradise.'

Luke 23:39–43

The words of Jesus

Heaven and earth will pass away, but my words will never pass away.

Luke 21:33

Acknowledgments

Photographs by British Trust for Ornithology: page 61;
Fritz Fankhauser: pages 16, 18, 30, 39, 40, 79, 83, 85, 89,
91; Fisons Fertilizer Division: page 28 and endpapers;
Philip Gardner: page 76; Sonia Halliday Photographs:
F.H.C. Birch, page 43, Sonia Halliday, pages 13, 20, 27,
32, 34, 45, 52, 56, 65, 67, 72, 86, Jane Taylor, 11, 36, 48,
54, 58, 68, 74; Alan Hutchinson Library: pages 23, 71,
Robin Constable, page 25; Paul Kay: page 80; Lion
Publishing: David Alexander, pages 14, 62, Jon
Willcocks, page 46.

Cover photograph by Robin Bath